U.S. MILITARY
TECHNOLOGY

U.S. MILITARY WARSHIPS

by Barbara Alpert

CONTENT CONSULTANT:
RAYMOND L. PUFFER, PHD
HISTORIAN, RET.
EDWARDS AIR FORCE BASE HISTORY OFFICE

READING CONSULTANT:
BARBARA J. FOX
READING SPECIALIST
PROFESSOR EMERITA
NORTH CAROLINA STATE UNIVERSITY

CAPSTONE PRESS
a capstone imprint

Blazers is published by Capstone Press,
1710 Roe Crest Drive, North Mankato, Minnesota 56003.
www.capstonepub.com

Library of Congress Cataloging-in-Publication Data
Alpert, Barbara.
  U.S. military warships / by Barbara Alpert.
  p. cm. — (Capstone blazers: U.S. military technology)
  Includes bibliographical references and index.
  Audience: Grades K to 3.
  ISBN 978-1-4296-8441-5 (library binding)
  ISBN 978-1-62065-213-8 (ebook PDF)
1. Warships—United States—Juvenile literature. I. Title.
VA55.A753 2013
359.8'30973—dc23   2012000997

Summary: Describes the warships used by the U.S. military.

Editorial Credits
Brenda Haugen, editor; Kyle Grenz, designer; Laura Manthe, production specialist

Photo courtesy of General Dynamics Bath Iron Works, 13; U.S. Navy Photo, 17, 28-29, by MC3
Colby K. Neal, cover (bottom), MCSN Matthew J. Haran, cover (top), MC2 Eric S. Garst, 22-23,
MC2 James R. Evans, 6-7, MC2 Jay C. Pugh, 18-19, MC2 Mark R. Alvarez, 21, MC3 John Philip
Wagner Jr., 9, MC3 Patrick Gearhiser, 14, MCC Bill Mesta, 26-27, MCSN Adam K. Thomas, 25,
MCSN James R. Evans, 5, PH2 Luke Williams, 10

Artistic Effects
deviantart.com/Salwiak, backgrounds

Printed in the United States of America in
Stevens Point, Wisconsin.
032012   006678WZF12

TABLE OF CONTENTS

POWER AT SEA

The oceans are home to hundreds of U.S. military warships. These ships form the most powerful fighting force afloat.

U.S. warships move troops and weapons into battle zones. They guard U.S. borders. They are ready for action if a war begins.

CHAPTER 1

THE BIGGEST AND BOLDEST

Huge aircraft carriers lead the action. They are more than 1,000 feet (305 meters) long. An aircraft carrier's **flight deck** can hold up to 85 aircraft. Each warship is home to about 5,000 crew members.

flight deck—the top deck of an aircraft carrier; planes use the flight deck to take off and land

flight deck

The crew of an aircraft carrier can launch or land one plane every 25 seconds!

A carrier's **missiles** can attack in any direction. The Phalanx defense system shoots down enemy missiles that get too close to the ship.

missile—an explosive weapon that can travel long distances

CHAPTER 2

SEARCH AND DESTROY

Destroyers travel on their own or as part of an aircraft carrier group. Destroyers shoot down enemy aircraft. They use **torpedoes** to destroy enemy submarines.

torpedo—an underwater missile

hull

FACT Destroyers are designed for speed. Their narrow **hulls** cut through giant waves.

hull—the main body of a boat

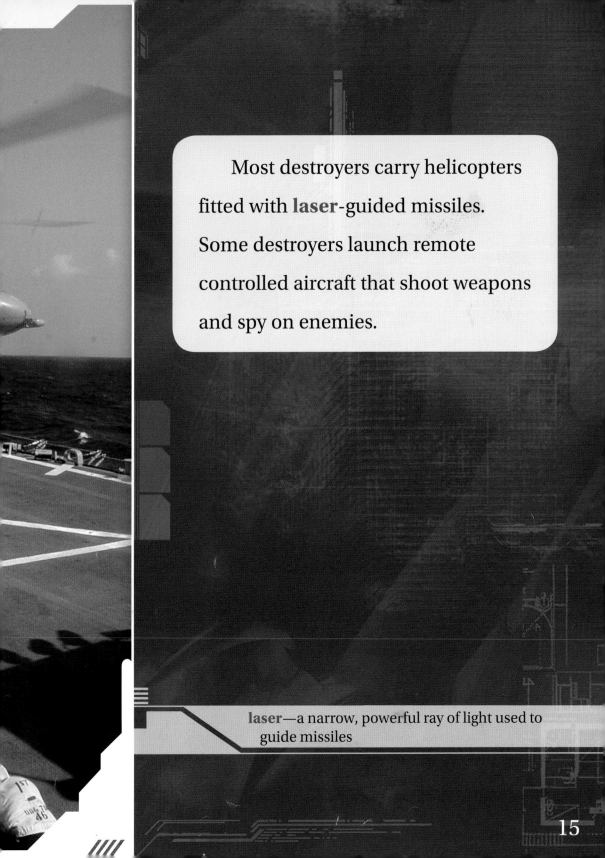

Most destroyers carry helicopters fitted with **laser**-guided missiles. Some destroyers launch remote controlled aircraft that shoot weapons and spy on enemies.

laser—a narrow, powerful ray of light used to guide missiles

CHAPTER 3

CRUISE INTO DANGER

Cruisers are built for battle. They respond quickly to threats at sea and in the air. Cruisers carry Tomahawk missiles.

A Tomahawk missile can destroy a target 1,500 miles (2,414 kilometers) away.

Tomahawk
missile

Cruisers carry helicopters called Seahawks. Each Seahawk helicopter can lift up to 3 tons (2.7 metric tons) of equipment and bring it to shore.

 Seahawks attack enemy subs and perform sea rescues.

CHAPTER 4

ON SEA AND ON LAND

Amphibious assault ships carry troops and cargo across oceans. They send boats onto beaches to get Marines and equipment to battle zones.

amphibious—able to work on land and in the water

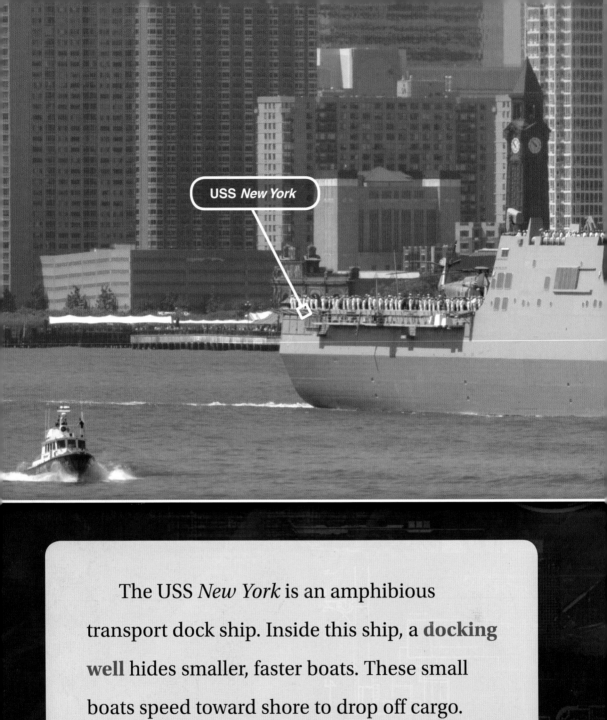

USS *New York*

The USS *New York* is an amphibious transport dock ship. Inside this ship, a **docking well** hides smaller, faster boats. These small boats speed toward shore to drop off cargo.

docking well—a large space within a ship where cargo and vehicles are loaded and unloaded

The hull of the USS *New York* contains 7.5 tons (6.8 metric tons) of steel from the fallen World Trade Center buildings in New York. On September 11, 2001, the Word Trade Center buildings were destroyed by terrorists.

CHAPTER 5

SMALL SHIPS, COOL JOBS

Frigates patrol the oceans to stop pirates and other criminals. They also use **sonar** to track enemy subs deep underwater.

sonar—a device that uses sound waves to find underwater objects

 Frigates carry guns that can destroy a target up to 6 miles (9.7 km) away.

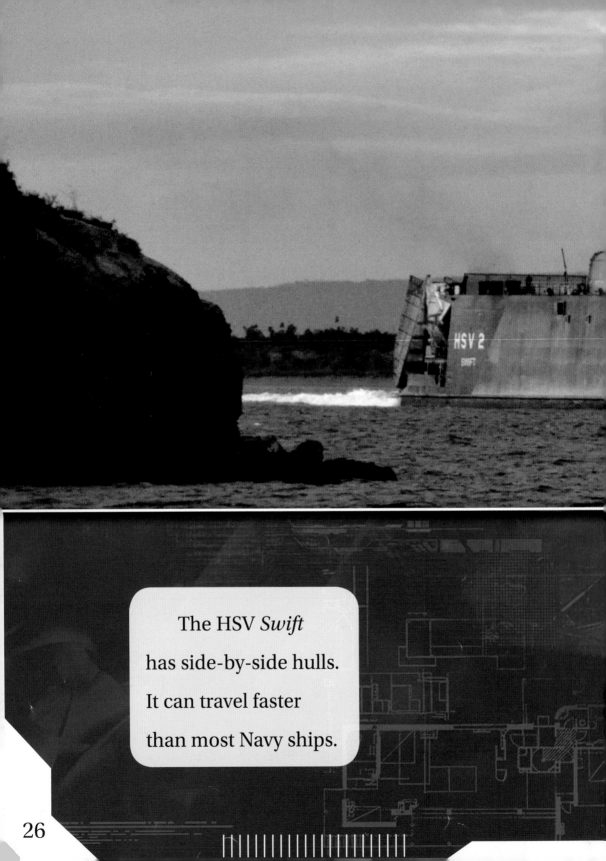

The HSV *Swift* has side-by-side hulls. It can travel faster than most Navy ships.

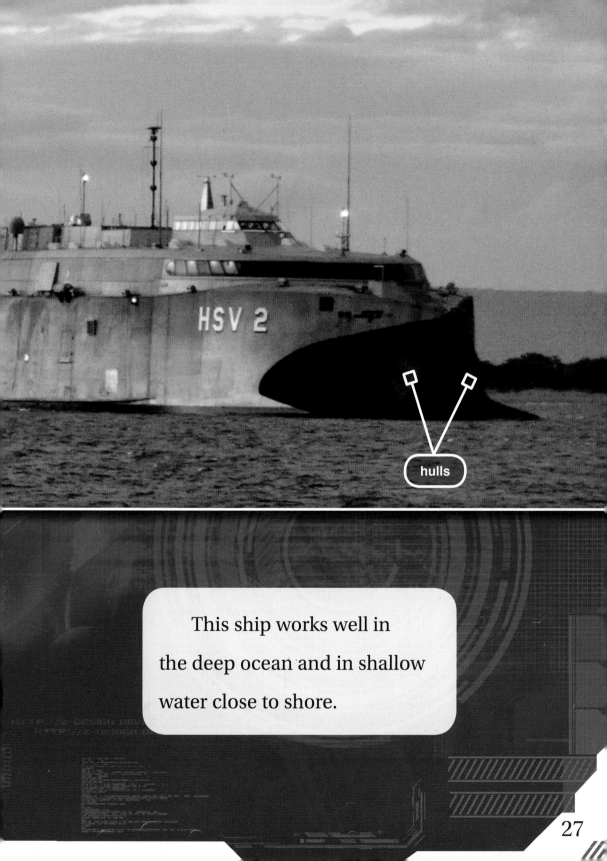

hulls

This ship works well in the deep ocean and in shallow water close to shore.

CHAPTER 6

WHAT'S NEXT?

By 2015 aircraft carriers will use a new **catapult** launch system to send fighter jets into battle.

A modern navy needs high-tech warships with the newest tools.

catapult—a device for launching an airplane from the deck of a ship

GLOSSARY

amphibious (am-FI-bee-uhs)—able to work on land and in the water

catapult (KAT-uh-puhlt)—a device for launching an airplane from the deck of a ship

docking well (DAH-king WEL)—a large space within a ship where cargo and vehicles are loaded and unloaded

flight deck (FLYTE DEK)—the top deck of an aircraft carrier; planes use the flight deck to take off and land

hull (HUHL)—the main body of a boat

laser (LAY-zur)—a narrow, powerful ray of light used to guide missiles

missile (MISS-uhl)—an explosive weapon that can travel long distances

sonar (SOH-nar)—a device that uses sound waves to find underwater objects

torpedo (tor-PEE-doh)—an underwater missile

READ MORE

Alvarez, Carlos. *Arleigh Burke Destroyers.* Military Machines. Minneapolis: Bellwether Media, 2010.

Jackson, Kay. *Navy Ships in Action.* Amazing Military Vehicles. New York: PowerKids Press, 2009.

Tagliaferro, Linda. *Who Lands Planes on a Ship?: Working on an Aircraft Carrier.* Wild Work. Chicago: Raintree, 2011.

INTERNET SITES

FactHound offers a safe, fun way to find Internet sites related to this book. All of the sites on FactHound have been researched by our staff.

Here's all you do:

Visit *www.facthound.com*

Type in this code: 9781429684415

Super-cool stuff!

Check out projects, games and lots more at
www.capstonekids.com

INDEX